VIA Folios 127

What My Father Taught Me

What My Father Taught Me

Maria Giura

BORDIGHERA PRESS

Library of Congress Control Number: 2017959138

Printed in the United States.

Published by
BORDIGHERA PRESS
John D. Calandra Italian American Institute
25 West 43rd Street, 17th Floor
New York, NY 10036

VIA FOLIOS 127
ISBN 978-1-59954-122-8

Contents

Note to the Reader

W hen my sisters and I were growing up, our mother and father owned a pastry shoppe in Brooklyn where we watched them create beautiful things. My father made the pastries, the cookies, the *cremolata*, the lemon ices, the multi-tiered wedding cakes; my mother made everything to display and package them all: the trays and baskets wrapped in shiny cellophane, the window displays with flowers and garland, the showcases with cookies lined up like delectable soldiers. They worked fourteen hour days, served thousands of customers. All my father had was a fifth grade education. He had emigrated from the Basilicata region of Italy when he was eighteen. The night before he was supposed to show up to his first day as a contractor's apprentice, he said to himself, "That's not my work." Instead he got a job at a bakery where he met my sixteen-year-old mother who had emigrated when she was eight from a small town in the northeastern section of Sicily near Messina. Two and half years later on the day before Valentine's Day, they married.

Over the course of the next sixteen years, they made a business together and four daughters with eyes as blue as theirs. Sadly, my father believed that except for providing for us, it was our mother's job to raise us. After many years of grappling with my father's emotional absence, the title poem of this collection came to me. I started with the truth—he hadn't been around enough to teach me what I needed to know—but then it showed me another: he gave bread the way he knew how, stayed still long enough to make something satisfying every day.

The theologian C.S. Lewis said, "God loved us into existence." Things are loved into existence too. That's what my mother and father did. Even though they wouldn't consider themselves artists—at least not in the traditional sense—I know that's what they are and what they passed onto me. Because of their vision and tenacity, and because I watched close up as they lost themselves in what they made, I had the chance to figure out what I was supposed to make. This collection of memory poems is the beginning, and it's dedicated to the both of them:

to my mother, JM, and to my father, A. Giura,
for the gift of my life and the complicated sweetness you created

Poetry is not an expression of the party line. It's that time of night, lying in bed, thinking what you really think, making the private world public, that's what the poet does.

ALLEN GINSBERG

Part I

WHAT MY FATHER TAUGHT ME

My father never taught me
how to fish or play ball or dance,
how to do repairs in the house
or talk to a repair man
so I wouldn't get taken for a fool.
He never taught me how to change oil
or a tire or even windshield wiper fluid.
He never read me a bedtime story
or asked me about school.

In the morning when I sat on his lap
he'd kiss my hair and call me Bella,
but when I tried to tell him something,
he'd look at the clock,
jump up and nearly drop me.
After he and my mother separated,
when it was his day to take me and Annie
he'd sometimes cancel,
leaving us in our dresses and barrettes,
holding hands.

I'm not sure I can finish this poem.
What do fathers teach their daughters?

He gave what he could: headlock kisses,
18 karat gold,
the newest electronic gadgets.
He wrote to us on layered birthday cakes
he made with his hands,
our names in delicate pink icing
in his squared European handwriting.
He held me high in his arms
on that one vacation to Italy with my mother
when I was four and clung to him

in St. Mark's Square
afraid of the pigeons;
held his hand on my leg
when I was atop an elephant at the zoo,
my lips pursed with fear.

Years later, whenever I visit him
and my step-mother, he always asks me,
"How's the car running?
How many miles?"
To this day, he brings my mother
sfingi and *zeppole* on her name day,
loaves of bread and seven-layers
anytime he's in the neighborhood,
asks me when I speak to him on the phone,
"How's Mamma?"

The same bakery that stole my father from us
gave me a man
who could pay attention long enough
to make something beautiful,
who helped me to
grow up

and write about him.

SFOGLIATELLE

My father's dream was to work hard
and make a lot of money,
to have customers come in droves and buy
dozens of pastries,
so the salesgirls—including my mother—
would have to pull out the largest boxes
and have hands quick enough
for the electric tying machine.

His dream came true.
People all over Brooklyn circled the block
that bordered Borough Park
to bring pastries for their Sunday visiting
and to order three-tiered wedding cakes.

But occasionally there was a customer
who'd come in for just one *sfogliatelle*,
the most expensive and complicated pastry to make.
It was usually an old man
whose clothes were as bent as he.
The salesgirl would lift it from the showcase
with a piece of wax paper
and place it in a crisp, white paper bag
that she slapped against her thigh to open.

Smelling the sale from the back,
my father would step into the doorway,
and glare at the man,
the cost and labor rolling out in his head.
He'd wipe the back of his greased hand
against his mouth, watch the man leave
with the *sfogliatelle*, cursing him as he went.

TWO SIDES OF THE LIVING ROOM

On one side,
Papa's blue recliner
where, after fourteen hour days,
he'd conk out,
his limp arm across me like a rail.

Where my mother placed
the furnishings he bought
without asking her—
the 18 x 22 portrait of the Pope,
the life-sized leopard statue,
the dark Venetian mural
that scared me
despite its slivers of light.

Where I sat on
the long, L shaped couch
trying to write their fighting away,

and my father popped the cork
on New Year's champagne
as he watched me and my sisters dance

to the other side
with its crushed velvet love seat
and enormous pale-blue breakfront
that he and my mother bought together.

Where in pretty A-line dresses,
she pulled out scotch and Mario Lanza
for friends and family and Papa's compari,
and arranged her favorite
porcelain knickknacks
including a small St. Michael slaying the devil.

Where my sisters and I
tore into Christmas gifts
and belted out *I Think I Love You*,
where we let Papa kiss us with his stubbly face.

Where we learned to pull out the microphone,
even though it was always broken,
and sing.

PAPA'S HEARING

I think about the
World War II Italy
of your childhood:
the shrieking air raids,
the nights that Nonna
sent you into the black
to scrounge for food.
Seven or eight,
but the oldest of three
with Nonno off at war,
you were as good as man.

I think about how
you left the fifth grade
to work with Nonno as a blacksmith,
scorching and beating metal,
hammering shoes onto horses' feet,

and about the noise that followed
you to America,
all the years that you and Mommy
owned the pastry shoppe
with its grinding industrial-strength mixers
and hissing walk-in-freezer,
the phone ringing off the hook.

When I call you now
you yell into the phone,
and I yell back
but you still can't hear me,
the soccer game blasting in the background.

I think about the noise
that has surrounded your life,

how it has deafened you
when all I ever wanted
was for you to hear my voice.

EARTHLY FATHER

My mother called last week to tell me that my father visited,
brought *zeppole* and *sfingi* for her name day, St. Joseph's Day.
And would you believe he sat down long enough
to have a cup of coffee? she told me over the phone.
He even wanted to see the basement,
because he forgot what it looked like.
My mother and father, divorced for over twenty years,
both remarried years ago though his visits are not unusual.
He stops off when he makes a pastry delivery
to a nearby restaurant or to visit his father's grave,
stops at my mother's to bring pizza,
panettone, cheese cakes.

For the first time in a long time, Papa leaves me money.
There's a surprise waiting for you with your mail
when you visit next, my mother says.
I smile at the thought of my mother and father in her kitchen—
her making coffee, his bringing pastries, his leaving me money.
He continues to love the only way he's ever known how.
When I call him to thank him, he begins to say *bacieto*, kisses,
but then stops, embarrassed.

I think about the fact that my father has never told me he loves me
and about the two one hundred dollar bills
waiting for me. I know he loves me without the words,
because he has never needled me, not once, even though
he is an Italian father, that I am not married.
Because he asks me every time he walks me to my car
when I have visited him how the car is running,
how many miles it has,
the same questions every time, his way of making a connection.

I think of St. Joseph and my father who's far from a saint
and suddenly they are not so unalike,

both men shadows to me my whole life,
men who make me doubt that I am seen
who stand there even though I cannot see them,
and worry if I have enough money,
worry if I am safe.

FATHER'S DAY

I want the family I do not have—

my mother and father lasting
beyond my ninth birthday.

I want to belong to two parents
who still belong to each other,
who I could go to
in a room in the same house
where my father wouldn't shake
my mother's hand the way he does now
as if they'd never conceived me.

I want to be one of those young trees
just planted,
whose trunks, thin as rulers,
are anchored on both sides
by stakes driven into the earth
and cable so tight
not even a strong wind can undo.

IN THIS ROOM

My nephew Jacob
who calls Grandpa Bob, Pabob,
wakes at 6:45 a.m.,
then does what he never does,
falls back asleep.
It's the quiet after his rumbling
that wakes and leads me
to my mother and stepfather's room
one last time.

I've always knocked softly,
but today I barely tap.

It's like church beyond this door.

Once inside, I walk slowly,
trying to stop time,
the two of them
still together
in this room.

When Bob realizes I'm there,
he struggles his head off the pillow—
a toothless smile
spreads like a baby's across his thin face.

What are you doing up?
he asks. *We had a date,* I remind him
as my mother slips out;
my presence means
she can make coffee without guilt.

I move the upholstered chair
with the fine hem

flush against the hospice bed
and reach my hand through the bars
as close as possible
to his without touching it
until he reaches for mine,
then I latch on.

Your feelings for God
are rubbing off on me
he says.

I'm going to miss you, I whisper.

I'm going to be with you,
I'm going to be with you more,
straining his head off the pillow again.

I want him to explain
this tenet of my faith
that I recite so well,
but at that moment Jacob comes in
stepping carefully where he would usually barrel.
Even he, three years old with blankie in tow,
knows it is holy in this room.

PRAYING YOU

Whenever I pray for someone,
I try to picture them in their environs—
a bedroom, an office, a car,
a favorite chair,
a messy desk.

It helps to have something tangible
when I whisper them to Him
or the Blessed Mother
as if they don't know of who I speak.

But with this prayer, this time, for you
in the days before summer in the year 2002
characterized by weather that has been confused—
warm winter, chilly spring
flowers premature, then die—

it's not enough to picture
you in your big boat of a Cadillac
and pray your name.
I picture your spine,
your right hip,
your lung where they found the tumors

and try my best to lift you up.

THREE YEARS TODAY

When my stepfather first met my mother, he kept
an index card in his breast pocket
with my and my sisters' names
and a detail or two, so he wouldn't mix us up.
Next to my name, he wrote: *writer*.

I think about the desk he assembled
for me that I bought at Sears
and the night he, my mother and I
knelt scrambled on my bedroom floor
how we, really he, went to work—
my mother and I wanting it done
before we'd begun
like after dinner
when she swept under his chair
while he still chewed his food.

He thumbed the instruction manual with care,
pulled his glasses higher on his nose
while we sighed about the August heat.

He approached
his toolbox like an artist.
Directed us to separate by size
the planks of wood
and the screws in clear, sealed packages.
Told us to hold the pieces of wood snug
so he could screw them together tightly,
moved his hands over the wood
with the same precision
as he did when hoisting
the jib and mainsails on his boat.

I didn't know that two years later,

in the fall, he would die nor that
the desk would follow me
to a writing program,
that it would be all I had left of his hands.

The last thing he wrote me
was a birthday card
the month before he died.
In handwriting that was wobbly and gaunt
with cancer, he wrote
To the writer of my life.

NO IDEA

I had no idea when I was young
that You'd always longed for me,
that I am the beloved
in the Song of Songs,

your Israel.

No idea
You'd known my name
for all eternity
before You whispered
it in my mother's ears
as she held me the first time,

that when she sang
Close to You,
it was You
who put the song
in her heart.

Or that every time
my father let me fall
You caught me.

No idea when I went
to weddings by myself,
watched bride and groom
and cried,
that I was aching for heaven,

that You ached for me first.

Or that You'd permit pain,
so I'd moan for You in the dark.

I had no idea
You'd never leave me alone,
that while I spent years
giving myself away,
You were saving me.

No idea even though
I kissed Your cross,
beheld Your face in Veronica's cloth,
how much You suffered for me.

I had no idea
I'd become one of them,
the Marys,
bathing Your feet with tears,
shouting Your name at the empty tomb.

BRIDGE

Driving on the Belt Parkway
on a brisk, winter night,
the Verrazano ascends
from Bay Ridge, a perfect arch
over the Narrows.

Gracing the barges
and potholes below,
the cables fall
like a necklace of white gold
stretching between towers
that rise from the water
like a woman's shoulders.
Each light's a diamond strung
between Forts Hamilton and Wadsworth,
but inside its mortar,
men fell to a different death.

It appears as the parkway bends west
from the places of my childhood
that are no longer there—
like *Nellie Bly* Amusement Park
where thrill unfurled from a wide spool of tickets,
and being a few yards above ground
was enough to soar.

I peer up at lights even more intense
against the season's frigid sky,
lean closer to the windshield
like trying to read a highway sign
when almost past it. This is my exit—
the place this Bridge exacts for me
where origin, like beams,
sustains the crossing.

CHRISTMAS IN DYKER HEIGHTS

Inside our bay window, the marble sill
became a stable with fake snow
and plastic replicas of the Nativity
illuminated by giant colored bulbs
except for Jesus dim
until midnight on Christmas Eve.
This Family and the one inside

faced east towards 13th Avenue.

This was years before
60 Minutes reported on the line of cars
winding the blocks to see
houses wild with lights,

when the ones strung above the avenue
were enough to cast out darkness

and whose stores below
carried the names of legends
—*Joe Torre, Mona Lisa*—
and were small enough
to sell fresh
especially in the days before the Eve:
chestnuts, *finocchio*,
bags of shellfish bursting
like a net at morning's end,

where your need was known
before you spoke it
as if inside St. Bernadette's
whose votives danced crimson
to the sound of whispered intentions.

This part of Brooklyn that never had
a train storm through—
like the R along 4th, the El on 86th—
where maybe time can slow
if only in the blink of this poem,
long enough for you
to reach your stop,
which like an heirloom
appreciates through the long absence.

LEARNING TO TALK

When I was little
I was taught not
to speak when someone else was,
so I watched the mouths
of my family as they
passed salt and pepper
across the kitchen table

waiting for my turn
that never seemed to come.

Many years later in my twenties
I developed a habit
of finishing people's sentences
just for them to be done,
to hear myself speak.

Maybe that's why I became a writer,
before I knew how to write,
scribbling on anything I could find—

my mother's high school yearbook,
the walls in Zia's apartment,
the order forms from the pastry shoppe.

The best surface of all
was my mother's pale, fleshy earlobes
better than the cushion of any thick paper.
There in her lap with pen in my hand,
I hoped my words would reach her ears.

ON THE BACK OF DAS DORIS' BIKE

One day when I was about six, Das Doris who lived upstairs
took me out on her bicycle—
the big-girl kind with banana handle bars
and tassels that flew as she pedaled. She lifted me up on the back,
told me to keep my legs apart,
away from the wheel. Then she got on and I wrapped my arms
around her narrow waist,
pointed my legs out to the sides,
my whole body stiff with determination and self-control
as she steered us down
our steep block, her long black hair
blowing in my face,
my stomach flying the way it did on rides.
Remember to keep your legs away from the wheel, she yelled.
I am, I yelled back, the air eating our words.
As she turned onto 12th Avenue,
I felt so free that I threw my head back
let my face feel the rush of air.
Two blocks later she veered onto 86th Street
with its four lane traffic
as I continued to cling excitedly
to this teenage girl with almond eyes.
Before we could get to 11th Avenue
my legs began to tire, slip,
fall closer to the wheel.
I pulled them apart, tried with all my might
to keep them that way, but they wouldn't listen
especially my right leg that kept dropping, dropping
until it got so close
the spokes snatched up my ankle and swallowed.
I screamed, but the cars were so loud
that Doris didn't hear. I don't remember
if I hit her on the back, just that my body
must have keeled into hers,

we must have wound up
like a shipwreck in front of a row of mother-daughters.
She must have undone my foot,
pressed down on the bleeding,
brushed away my tears.

So much time has passed since then.
A faint scar remains, a sliver of a line
stretched over the years,
reminding me of what can sometimes happen when I let go.

GIRL SCOUT

One day after a Brownie meeting
in the basement of St. Bernadette's Rectory
when I was in third or fourth grade,
I stole for the first time.

We had just finished making
Mother's Day gifts,
pictures on tissue thin paper
with special magic markers
that our leaders transferred onto
white, Coronet-type plates.

I drew a rainbow,
and tulips and a heart in the middle
and wrote *Happy Mother's Day, Mommy*
above the rainbow
and *Love, Maria* beneath it .

I was in my brown jumper
with orange, criss-cross tie
and brown sash with some patches and pins,
the younger version of the Girl Scout
in our handbook, pretty and proud in her Kelly-green
dress looking at herself in the mirror,
the page I kept coming back to,
skipping over the chapters about tying a knot
or some other boyish, outdoorsy task.

I don't remember who the lip gloss belonged to,
maybe Linda, my nemesis,
who cried until we made her the Blessed Mother
in the Christmas play we staged.

There was no one left in the room,

and it was sitting on the table,
not just any lip gloss,
but the thick, fat kind with a ball top
that tasted like strawberry.

I slipped it into my pocket
quietly, expertly,
and brought it home
with my Mother's Day plate
under my arm.

IDOL

Girls my age had posters of Scott Baio
on their bedroom walls,
but my idol was Roseanne Scarmadella
who anchored the evening news
and had chestnut brown hair like mine.

I thought if she could do it, maybe I could to,
even though I didn't speak until I was three
and was afraid to talk in front of people.
When I was small, I took out the microphone
when no one was looking,
and paraded up and down our living room,
dreaming I was saying something captivating
to thousands of people who loved me.

I wanted to like Edward R. Murrow High School,
with its enormous course offerings
and TV studio, its great newspaper
and students of all races and religions.
I wanted to go to college
for broadcasting,
be on the news, successful,
but I felt lost and anxious
in the cloud of four thousand students.

I wanted and didn't want to transfer
halfway through freshman year
into a Catholic school
where most of the girls
were Italian-American
like me.

MR. STANZA

Mr. Dom Stanza, who lived in Bed Sty
but commuted to Dyker Heights, was
the only male teacher in our school
of lay women and nuns.

He hiccupped a lot,
was always red in the face,
and sucked on sour balls.
The rumor was he drank too much.
I didn't notice.

He taught us Orwell's
Animal Farm and *1984* and
Golding's *Lord of the Flies*,
sat on the windowsill,
his feet up on a chair,
with the brick houses on 83th Street
like an urban Rockwell behind him.

One day he told us
that we should never think
too much of ourselves,
that if someone looks like they're staring at us,
they might just be burping.

He was six foot,
with a gut that rolled over his pants.
He sweat moons of perspiration through
his polyester shirts that he wore with no ties,
unlike the women
who were neater, proper, like our science teacher Mrs. T
who loved my friend Cetta
because she was great at science,
but seemed to have little interest in me.

Maybe she thought there were already
too many girl-writers
(or maybe I thought too much of myself).

Mr. Stanza was the only teacher
who didn't care if you crossed out
or if your homework looked like
it *had* been chewed;
who taught us
that we could be terribly imperfect
and still be *good.*
The teacher who awarded me
the English prize,
whose own last name
means a measure of poetry,
and in Italian, means room,
both of which he gave me
all those years ago.

CHRIST IN CONCRETE

It was spring of sophomore year,
Literature of New York
with Mr. G.
who was so handsome
my all-girls school buzzed.
He wore glasses and a three piece suit,
was smart and soft-spoken.

We read Albert Halper's "Scab!"
about the taxi unions
and JD Salinger's *Catcher in the Rye*,
but it was Pietro di Donato's characters
who made me cry:

Geremio, the brick-layer,
a husband and father of seven
who was crucified in cement on Good Friday
by Job with a capital J.

Paul, his twelve year old son,
who buckled from the weight
of supporting his mother and siblings
and lost all faith in God.

Father John, the parish priest,
who handed off a slice of cake
when Paul knocked at the rectory
for real food.

I still remember the bleeding strawberries
sliding off the white angel food,
the sick feeling in my stomach.
I remember my anger,
the tears rising up the inside of my nose.

I remember thinking,
where are the other Italian-American writers,
why is no one else teaching them?

If I saw Mr. G. today, I'd thank him
for the book that changed my life,
made me care for more than my little world.
I'd thank him for making me go in search
of the other di Donatos.

If I saw him Mr. G. today, I'd tell him
I had a crush on him too.

AT FIFTEEN

At fifteen I got my first job at a restaurant
a block away from Macy*s.
I took the subway
to Manhattan,
emerging from Penn Station
in my skirts
on summer mornings that were hot by nine,
to ring up plates of baked ziti and eggplant parmigiana
for the lunch crowd.

I was so excited—
clutching my pocketbook,
smoothing my skirt—
until I turned the corner
and saw the men
crawling from the backs of their trucks.

"Beautiful blue eyes, baby. Where'd you get *t...h...o...s...e*?"
one of them hissed,
while the others smacked
the air with vulgar kisses.
I felt like the woman
in the photograph
American Girl in Italy,
her eyes downcast,
gripping her scarf.

I kept my head up,
careful not to look
them in the eye,
but smiled,
so I wouldn't seem rude.

THE FIRST TIME I SMOKED

The first time I smoked,
I was at The Nautical,
a bar on Fort Hamilton Parkway,
that didn't proof.
Anything to look cool,
especially in front of Shawn N.
who said he'd take me to the senior prom
then cancelled a week before.

Until then, I'd worn no make-up,
hardly rolled up my skirt,
went to Prayer Group every Tuesday morning
where a Sister of Saint Joseph
lit a candle, read from Scripture.
I loved the way the flame
burned through the bland smell
of that convent room
where I was afraid
one of the girls with teased hair
and ankle-bracelet chain
might spot me.

When my friend Cetta,
who'd known me since I was eight,
caught me smoking one day,
she said, "I was so disappointed."

It was the easy thing to do—
to lit up,
to curse,
to make-out with boys who didn't buy me drinks—
anything to try and deny the girl inside
who thought she wasn't pretty or worthy enough,
who snuck around seeking Christ.

BROOKLYN ACADEMY OF MUSIC

Mom, do you remember that day
all of us outside the
Brooklyn Academy of Music,

your graduation from
Physical Therapy school
the same spring I graduated
high school?

You, with
that sparkle in your eyes,
beating the odds—going back to school
at the age of thirty-nine with four daughters.
The voices of overly cautious others—
She's taking too much on herself again—
blending with your own doubt—
I haven't been in school in twenty years.

I remember that day, Mom,
your face so full of smile
and your yellow tassel
swinging in the June air.
You among your bohemian classmates
with their long, crimped hair
and leather sandals sticking out
from graduations gowns.

All of us posed around your brown Cutlass,
with Grandpa sitting in the passenger seat
because of the leg he lost seventeen years earlier,
his beaming face framed by the open window.
His youngest daughter would now follow
other men around reprimanding
them for using their canes improperly

and talking about such things as gait.
(What does gait mean? I had to ask)

You in your cap and gown
and me in my striped linen dress,
but your studies involved sacrifice.

I kissed my first kiss on the front stoop
the summer you took Anatomy & Physiology.
As thoughts of wedding taffeta rushed through me,
you were buried under a box of bones
laid out on our kitchen table.
You recited the names out loud
like the pisiform. You pressed my hand
hard, right under the pinky to make me feel
mine. You practiced massages on us, eager
volunteers we were for your hands
that had wrapped thousands of cookie trays
all those years in the pastry shoppe.

Do you remember, Mom, all the people—
most of them who towered over your 4'11" frame—
now looking up to you for help? The stroke patients,
the accident victims, the elderly, the children with
developmental delays, the athletes who hurt themselves?

Do you realize how you touched them, Mom,
with your hands and your compassion,
and the knowledge
that they would move again
when they didn't believe it?

Do you realize, Mom, that this daughter
feels pride right through her bones,

do you realize everything that started
that day outside the
Brooklyn Academy of Music?

Part II

MARCH

I'm tired of hearing people
complain about winter.
It's not that I don't love spring
with its first buds
and the cottony smell of the air,

but I feel like they're wishing life away,
and it's already moving too fast,
the years vanishing
like breath into cold air.

I want it to stay winter
as long as it is,
as long it needs to—
even though it means
swinging at the snow piles on my car roof
on tippy toe in sopped boots
for the tenth time.

I want to eat my breakfast,
looking out at silence—
the naked trees bearing white—
then later drive Forest Hill Road
where more of them form a canopy
like a scene from Currier & Ives.

By the end of the day,
the snow will melt
and trickle out the gutters
watering the soil
and the sleeping flowers
that are waiting
for just the right time
to burst into life.

ANNUNCIATION

He came to you like grace
the moment you said *Yes.*

Nine months later in
a gush of blood and joy, he came.

He came to you when Simeon
promised a sword would pierce your heart;

anytime he fell and scraped his knee,
he came.

He came to you when you
found him among the elders,

and years later when you
instructed he turn water into wine.

He came to you in agony
when you could do nothing but meet his eyes.

When he told you from the cross,
"Behold your son,"

and his dead body lay in your arms,
he came to you.

Once he'd resurrected,
with tongues of fire, he came.

He came to you,
when your life was over,

the Word made Flesh,

who had kicked inside you,

stretching, growing—
a shining, glorious Son.

LA PRIMAVERA

Every year at this time
I'm reminded
why I love spring.
I can bring the plants outside
and they'll survive,
can open the sliding glass door
and let in the sky.
The sounds that I strained
to hear all winter long
through sealed doors and windows
return to me
like the murmur of train that runs
through the back of Broome County
reminding me of the train tracks
in Grandma and Grandpa's backyard
in Roselle Park , New Jersey
all those years ago
where I rode my tricycle
that I was allowed to bring from Brooklyn
over the Goethals Bridge,

the murmur of train
that reminds me of those days
when I was still someone's granddaughter.

MAY FLOWERS

During May, the May of
Catholic school calendars,
when I was in grammar school
I used to bring flowers
from our yard
to the Blessed Mother.

My mother would clip
daffodils, tulips, irises.
I watched her pressed up against
the counter in our kitchen
with that no nonsense look on her face.
She fed their stems
with moistened paper towel,
wrapped them in foil
that she molded into the shape of a cone.

I presented them
to my teacher,
a woman,
as if I'd grown them myself.

Did my mother know
in her skilled arranging,
her fingers
moving expertly along
the stiff stems of flowers—
Did I know
in my girlish need
to be noticed and praised—
Did my teacher know
as she undid the flowers
in a vase,
placed them at her feet?

We saw a Queen, untouchable,
clothed in majestic blue
like a cloud
on our Church walls,
in our Italian art.

Did we understand that
she who stood on a pedestal
in our cinder-block classrooms
with palms outstretched,
and whom we crowned
on a newly May night
was a young, Jewish girl
who knew the love of a man who
wanted to marry her,
the pain when he looked at her with confusion
before the dream?
A girl who knew
the faint feeling of morning sickness,
blood draining from her face,
her body exploding with Child?

Did we understand
this girl who craved her husband's touch—
that in the absence of their making love,
was the love they made—
that by her forties
she would be
widow,
mother of a murdered Son?

Did we see the woman
and not just the Lady?

Had we known her humanity
would our flowers
have ever been enough?

ROSES

Outside my door,
two small rose plants
grow in the shadow
of a long, narrow pine,

the only place there's room.

Far cry from the luxurious,
long- stemmed dozen
of Valentine's Day,

their petals and leaves
the size of a thumbnail
and smooth,
but struggling,
their thorns almost imperceptible.

No running streams here
and too far
from the sprinkler's nozzle
to be lavished
like the verdant lawn,
the emerald trees.

Small, side by side,
hardly noticeable
until you look.

They were a gift
from a friend,
these toiling plants
the rain does not forget.

OCTOBER SKY
(for E.H.)

A close friend sent a poem this morning
about the Florida sky
after a cleansing rain—
no clouds, just endless blue.
It was still raining in New York
well into the morning,
a low, thick sky of fog.
Yesterday we spoke
about my struggle to believe
I have what it takes to finish a memoir,
that what I remember *is* enough
to undo all the knots.
We spoke about my fears, my doubts,
until the sun cut through
one half of the sky
and turned it pale, pale blue,
large white clouds
crawling across,
grey only at the edges.

CROSS

I forget if my parents or godparents
gave me the gold cross I wore for my baptism
on that chilly November day
in Regina Pacis Shrine Church.
It was 18 karat
with etched design,
too long for a baby.

I put it on in high school,
took it off in college,
then put it on again ten years later
for my niece's christening,
promising to do better.

Sometimes I was faithful
wearing it outside my shirt
at the liberal university I worked at;
other times I concealed it under
a boat or turtle neck
relieved to keep Christ beneath my shirt.
Still, I never wanted to lose it,
but I lose so much of my jewelry
incessantly toying with their clasps.

Some years later on the way
back from another niece's communion
when my brother–in–law was driving,
I was playing with the cross
all the way from the Susquehanna River
to the Delaware Water Gap
when it finally slipped from my neck
into the deep recesses of the SUV.

When we combed the car, nothing;

it might have fallen into the clutch.
I could've bought a new cross,
someone did buy me a new cross,

but it wasn't the same
as the original
placed around my neck
when I was still too small
to play with something
so precious.

MERCY

On that last Mother's Day
before Grandma died,
I picked her up in New Jersey
having just come from Mass
where the air smelled of roses.

Behind her and Grandpa's four-family,
the soil was tilled for growing,
and the trees had found their bloom.
I tried to hold back the tears,
but they had begun again
the way they had when the priest
asked the mothers to stand
and I, over thirty, remained seated
not knowing how to feel anything
but self pity.

Inside, Grandma,
who had not seen me crying
since I was a little girl,
looked like one herself
waiting for me at the kitchen table
with her white, beauty parlor hair
and poplin dress that came to her knees,

Grandma, who never hugged you tight
but said your name
like she was crooning it,
who spoke to our clothes
as she ironed them—
bambinidittu, sweet little babies.
She always spoke in Sicilian,
the only language she knew,
with its Arabic endings,

the soft *u* at the end of words
like an embrace.

I'd have to ask my mother
to explain; then I'd respond
in careful textbook Italian
pausing to make sure I got it right,
trying so hard—
the way I always do—

while grandma
smiled, laughing, but never at me.
When she saw my face
she didn't ask why,
the way others do
who look confused
when I try to explain.
Instead, looking
at the Holy Family on the wall
then at me,
she said, *la Sagra Famigia*—
vai sempre alla Sagra Famigia,
compassion flooding her face so completely
it didn't matter that she didn't know
nor that I had no interpreter—
I finally understood
it was mercy
that had always been
her first language.

CROSSING NEW DORP LANE

One Friday night
when I was driving
on New Dorp Lane,
I saw Father Michael crossing the street
with an elderly couple.
He walked in between them
supporting them
as they crossed the lane
to Sedutto's Ice Cream.

He was a fifty-something Jesuit priest
who took a run-down retreat house
that was supposed to close
and turned it into a gem.
Yet, people had something
to complain about including me.

I wanted to stop Father and ask him where
his goodness would get him.
A Friday night with an elderly couple
who are not his parents
when at this point in his life
he could be at home with a wife,
and a couple of grandchildren
only a few years away?

I wanted to pull my car over,
and follow them in.
I wanted to tap him on the shoulder,
as he paid for their ice cream
—his in a cone, theirs in Dixie cups—
and ask him if he was happy,
ask him if it was worth it.

ROCKIN' EVE

It's New Year's
and we're at my sister's,
the ball already dropped,
the fire roaring,
Martini & Rossi still in our glasses.

Rockin' Eve is on in the background.
A split screen shows on one side
Carrie Underwood and Miley Cyrus
in crushed velour caps,
lyrics pouring from their mouths.
And on the other, Dick Clark
struggling to pull up his words
while thousands below him scream.

By now my nephews
have disappeared to the basement
with their toy guns.

Only the girls have stayed back to sing
around my niece's karaoke machine.

I draw close to them—
these girls
who share my DNA—
and sing
Life's what you make it, so let's make it rock
when I catch my sister's mother-in-law
stare at me from the couch.
I know her long enough—twenty years—
to know what she's thinking,

What a shame Maria never married.

She means well,
but her stare triggers the self-pity
I thought I had under control,
so I sing louder
trying to drown it out,
wishing it could be as easy as nine years old again—
not that everything at nine is easy.
Still, you can dance in a circle of girls
at a New Year's party,
throw your lungs into a pop song,
and really believe the lyrics.

PRAYER

I'm sitting on the floor
with my legs crisscrossed,
trying to imitate the mystics
that fill thick books
of Catholic saints,
imagining Jesus on the ottoman next to me.

I rest my arms
on my thighs,
my fingers in mudra position
but that feels itchy
so I open my hands
but that's not any better,
so I pick up *Living Faith*
open it up to today's gospel—
the Sermon on the Mount.
I repeat the second beatitude
like a mantra
blessed are you who are now hungry
for you will be satisfied
when the most recent man
I've dated—a screenwriter—
plays himself over in my head
as I beseech him
a litany of questions,
like, why would you take my hand in yours
over the tiramisu
then not call again?

It was the same night
he asked me which treatment
he should work on next, and
I told him definitely the one
called *The Liberator*,

about a woman he'd like Marisa Tomei to play
who needs help getting rid of men
who don't know what they want.

Five years after the screenwriter

I'm still asking the same questions,
this time of a man who asks me
the first time we go out
if I'll read his daughter's poetry,
and looks at me
like he doesn't want to see me go
then turns around and leaves.

I move through whys
like fingers over Rosary beads
except the one I should be asking:
Why am I dating
when I don't feel called to marriage?
I pray the phone will ring,
legs crisscrossed, forearms up,
hunger in my veins.

GOD BLESS THE GIURA HOME

Growing up, we had a plate
hanging in our kitchen,
God Bless the Giura Home,
with the famous profile of our Lord
from the Last Supper—
his hair shoulder length like a woman's,
his eyes piercing brown.

When I moved out at twenty-four,
my mother who hadn't been
a Giura in fifteen years,
said I could have it.

I put Jesus above the hallway closet
of my one-bedroom
where he watched
as I struggled with my calling,
opened my couch to men
I didn't love or trust.

Seven years later,
I entered a convent.

Along with the couch
and Fortunoff table,
I stored Jesus away and didn't find him, not really,
until three years later when, instead
of becoming a nun, I went for a Ph.D.
I put him over the entrance door
of another one bedroom, this time
in upstate New York. He watched
as I studied, taught,
wrote the first draft of a memoir
about me and him and the boys

I'd tried to substitute for him.

Four years later when I moved back to the city,
I broke the plate—
two cracks right through *Giura Home*—
though Jesus remained completely intact.
I tried to fix it with crazy glue,
but I only made it worse.
Now it sits in a file drawer
waiting for me to bring it,
the way I've finally brought myself,
to the one who knows what he's doing.

CRIES

If I could change one habit,
I'd wake when women with infants wake,
would rise in the dark
to sentences, sometimes whole paragraphs,
calling.

I'd go to my writing
as if it were a baby
like I did in a dream I had not long ago.
I was in a club,
when I heard an infant's tears
from a distant room
and knew she belonged to me.
I tried to move toward her,
but the crowd pressed in on me.
Panicked, I clawed my way
until I found her,
leaned over the crib,
brought her to my heart.

If I could change one habit,
I'd hear the urgency in words,
wouldn't let them cry
the way the parenting
books sometimes tell you to.
I'd throw off the covers,
trample the cold, dark mornings,
rush all the way to my keyboard
to stop the tears.

SLOW

No alarm clock or place to be,
just light pushing through the slats
and another day of writing ahead.
I bargain with myself,
a shorter shower,
a quicker breakfast
anything for just another ten minutes of sleep,
but then it's another and another
until the self-loathing pulls me
to the 3rd floor of the college library,
where I wrestle with sentences
in between picking my nails,
munching on chips and cookies
even though food's not allowed.

Maybe by the end of the day
I have something to show for myself,
but most days it's a crawl.
At night, struggling to sleep,
I repeat a prayer,
but my mind still buzzes,
Have I done enough?
Maybe a little more will tire me out.
Instead, I slip half a sleeping pill.

How much time have I wasted?
How much further ahead would I be?

Mothers and nuns rise early
for children and lauds,
but I, with no vow except to write,
remain in bed a little while longer.

THE DIAMETER OF LOVE

From my mother's pots and pans,
grand masterpieces arise:

marinaras and meat sauces,
lasagnas and soups,
stuffed eggplants and swai,
pizza rusticas, Easter breads

a different meal every day
for the last fifty years.

Meals she prepares at home
then packs in an insulated tote
to bring to the grandchildren.

She called me from my sister's recently.
Could I read her the raspberry biscotti recipe?
She knew most of it by heart,
just needed to check
if it was baking powder or soda,
how long each log of dough should be--

a recipe from the Sicilian cookbook
I bought her
that she has highlighted like a treasured text.

Her favorite passage from Scripture
is the multiplication of fishes and loaves
especially when Jesus saves the leftovers.
She says it's true, a small amount, with love,
becomes more than enough.

My mother, the most private person you'll ever meet,
never wanted that 50th birthday party we threw her,

gets self-conscious when she goes up to a counter to order something,

I can't go anywhere without someone saying,
How's your mom?
I love your mom.
Give your mom a hug.

My sister's neighbor
calls her Nonna, says,
"Your mother's so wise.
She's just one of the girls."

Where did I come from?

This daughter who's a Leo,
who enjoys recognition,
who earnestly writes her mother's recipes down,
then dumps vegetables into pasta
with only a little olive oil,

this daughter who's always trying so hard,
but not at cooking,
not at giving everything she has away.

PASQUALE

Pasquale, Patsy,
your name means Easter,

even in this dingy room
in Kaaterskill Care
where you lay, forty-seven,
your body worn and jaundiced
from cancer a second time.

We're here to say goodbye, cousin,
cuz, who I grew up with
watching Sesame Street
through the tiny white weave of our playpen,
then when we were a little older
Zoom and Electric Company.
We were even on Wonderama
singing *Kids Are People Too* on national TV,
wacka doo wacka doo wacka doo.

You're beside me at all my birthday parties,
at the kids' table,
dancing on the slippery linoleum floor
in my basement,
the two of us dressed in outfits
our mothers bought for us in Bunnyland
and the cone-shaped hats
the older kids refused to wear.

In the summer,
we splashed in
my small, blue plastic pool.

As we got older—
you with your School of Visual Arts degree

and me with my poems—
I wanted to start a greeting card line together.
You'd do the sketches;
I'd write the sentiments,

but marriage and a different religion
took you more than a hundred miles away.

You followed all the rules, Pasquale,
you stayed inside the lines,
but it didn't prosper you
the way Acts promises it will,
though what do I know?

You with your beautiful smile,
you never complained, not even now.
You just rolled your brown eyes.
Even your sarcastic wit could never be mean
(though you sometimes might have wanted it to).

In the end,
I don't think it matters to God
what name we give Him
as long as we believe; as long as we're good.
You do Pasquale; you *are*.
And now I know He's coming for you
to lift you from this place
and bring you home
where you will always be
young and healthy and unafraid;
where you will always smile
and roll your eyes and make your art;
where you will always be your daughters' father,
your siblings' brother-friend;

where you will always be your father's little prince,

and your mother's Pasquelino;

where it will always be

Easter.

TYLER, I'M SORRY

Tyler, I'm sorry
your mom picked me
to be your godmother,
this unmarried aunt
with no children of her own
who looks to you
like a son she didn't have.

You at 2.9 pounds, the smallest
of your siblings, who stayed in the n.i.c.u the longest
but who had the strongest lungs,
because you had to fight for your place
like I have, though for different reasons.

You who had low muscle tone
and early intervention,
who couldn't hold a pencil,
is now off to Stevens Institute for engineering.
When you were ten and we took a walk
through the World Financial Center,
I said, "One day you'll build something like this."

You have always been special, Tyler,
with that idiosyncratic mind.

You, with your Legos,
and snow globes
and the calligraphy you inherited from Pop-Pop.
You who likes origami,
and making tea and fencing,
who always says "*Thank you,*"
and "*How are you?*"

You who girls trust,

who dislikes sports,

who studies Chinese
instead of Spanish,
and wants to see Germany
more than Italy.

You who chose me as your hero,
compared me to Buddha,
told me, "*You're* happy, Aunt Maria."

One day sweetheart,
when you're building your skyscrapers,
will you come down
to hold my hand,
help this aunt across the street?

WHAT IF?

Every decision I make, I
wonder if I should have made the other:
if tails would have been better than heads.

Over a hundred
writers last night at the conference
dancing to a deejay that played
my favorite music.
I stayed in to watch
The Devil Wears Prada even
though I've seen it before,
even though I do this at home.

I wasn't sure I wanted
to do the work of fitting in.
There was also the large screen TV
and king size bed with 800 count sheets.

One day will I tell my younger self
that every decision she made was okay
even if it was the wrong one,
that everywhere she decided to stay or go
was good enough?

Or will I tell her
she should have
slipped her heels back on,
spritzed perfume on her neck,
and danced?

MARY

I like my Marys
when she's not being assumed,
coronated, glorified,
put on a shelf
like a china doll.

I like my Marys earthly,
with the Babe in her arms,
sandals firmly planted
in Nazareth

and her face
instead of demurely bowed,
blazing,
declaring to Elizabeth:
From this day all generations will call me blessed.

I like my Marys with long hair
and a headband,
her eyes fixed on the Baby,
on us,
like the statue
in the church near my sister's in Rochester,
that looks more flesh than plaster
and has no title or at least none
we can figure out.

I need my Marys human,
for when I look at her
I think there might be a chance
for me
pregnant with
every kind of fear,
every kind of dreaming.

In Gratitude

This book would not have been possible without Maria Mazziotti Gillan who helped me fall in love with poetry, whose workshops have taught me to "go to the cave" of my life and shine a light on it, and whose own poignant, courageous poems inspire me to tell the truth.

To Bordighera Press, especially Anthony Tamburri for his acceptance and support of my work, and Nick Grosso for his understanding and skill in producing such a visually appealing book.

To my mentor, Ed Hack, who has shown me, often line-by-line, word-by-word, *how* less is more. I am blessed and grateful.

To my sisters, my first and best friends, for sharing so much of this journey with me.

To all the persons who appear in my poems, human and divine, who have loved me, challenged me, or helped show me myself— sometimes all three.

Acknowledgments

Grateful acknowledgments to the editors of the following journals in which these poems first appeared: "The First Time I Smoked," *Presence: A Journal of Catholic Poetry,* 2018; "*Sfogliatelle,*" *Ovunque Siamo,* 2018; "Mary," *Italian Americana,* 2017; "Mr. Stanza," *Voices in Italian Americana,* 2017; "Tyler, I'm Sorry," *Paterson Literary Review,* 2017; "What My Father Taught Me," *Lips,* 2017; "Mercy," *Paterson Literary Review,* 2012; "Earthly Fathers," *Paterson Literary Review,* 2006; "May Flowers," *Voices in Italian Americana,* 2002; "Brooklyn Academy of Music," *Paterson Literary Review,* 2000.

GARY MORMINO. *Italians in Florida*. Vol 51. History. $15

GIANFRANCO ANGELUCCI. *Federico F*. Vol 50. Fiction. $15

ANTHONY VALERIO. *The Little Sailor*. Vol 49. Memoir. $9

ROSS TALARICO. *The Reptilian Interludes*. Vol 48. Poetry. $15

RACHEL GUIDO DE VRIES. *Teeny Tiny Tino's Fishing Story*. Vol 47. Children's Literature. $6

EMANUEL DI PASQUALE. *Writing Anew*. Vol 46. Poetry. $15

MARIA FAMÀ. *Looking For Cover*. Vol 45. Poetry. $12

ANTHONY VALERIO. *Toni Cade Bambara's One Sicilian Night*. Vol 44. Poetry. $10

EMANUEL CARNEVALI. *Furnished Rooms*. Vol 43. Poetry. $14

BRENT ADKINS. et al., Ed. *Shifting Borders. Negotiating Places*. Vol 42. Conference. $18

GEORGE GUIDA. *Low Italian*. Vol 41. Poetry. $11

GARDAPHÈ, GIORDANO, TAMBURRI. *Introducing Italian Americana*. Vol 40. Italian/American Studies. $10

DANIELA GIOSEFFI. *Blood Autumn/Autunno di sangue*. Vol 39. Poetry. $15/$25

FRED MISURELLA. *Lies to Live By*. Vol 38. Stories. $15

STEVEN BELLUSCIO. *Constructing a Bibliography*. Vol 37. Italian Americana. $15

ANTHONY JULIAN TAMBURRI, Ed. *Italian Cultural Studies 2002*. Vol 36. Essays. $18

BEA TUSIANI. *con amore*. Vol 35. Memoir. $19

FLAVIA BRIZIO-SKOV, Ed. *Reconstructing Societies in the Aftermath of War*. Vol 34. History. $30

TAMBURRI. et al., Eds. *Italian Cultural Studies 2001*. Vol 33. Essays. $18

ELIZABETH G. MESSINA, Ed. *In Our Own Voices*. Vol 32. Italian/American Studies. $25

STANISLAO G. PUGLIESE. *Desperate Inscriptions*. Vol 31. History. $12

HOSTERT & TAMBURRI, Eds. *Screening Ethnicity*. Vol 30. Italian/American Culture. $25

G. PARATI & B. LAWTON, Eds. *Italian Cultural Studies*. Vol 29. Essays. $18

HELEN BAROLINI. *More Italian Hours*. Vol 28. Fiction. $16

FRANCO NASI, Ed. *Intorno alla Via Emilia*. Vol 27. Culture. $16

ARTHUR L. CLEMENTS. *The Book of Madness & Love*. Vol 26. Poetry. $10

JOHN CASEY, et al. *Imagining Humanity*. Vol 25. Interdisciplinary Studies. $18

ROBERT LIMA. *Sardinia/Sardegna*. Vol 24. Poetry. $10

DANIELA GIOSEFFI. *Going On*. Vol 23. Poetry. $10

ROSS TALARICO. *The Journey Home*. Vol 22. Poetry. $12

EMANUEL DI PASQUALE. *The Silver Lake Love Poems*. Vol 21. Poetry. $7

JOSEPH TUSIANI. *Ethnicity*. Vol 20. Poetry. $12

JENNIFER LAGIER. *Second Class Citizen*. Vol 19. Poetry. $8

FELIX STEFANILE. *The Country of Absence*. Vol 18. Poetry. $9

PHILIP CANNISTRARO. *Blackshirts*. Vol 17. History. $12

LUIGI RUSTICHELLI, Ed. *Seminario sul racconto*. Vol 16. Narrative. $10

LEWIS TURCO. *Shaking the Family Tree*. Vol 15. Memoirs. $9

LUIGI RUSTICHELLI, Ed. *Seminario sulla drammaturgia*. Vol 14. Theater/Essays. $10

FRED GARDAPHÈ. *Moustache Pete is Dead! Long Live Moustache Pete!*. Vol 13. Oral Literature. $10

JONE GAILLARD CORSI. *Il libretto d'autore. 1860–1930*. Vol 12. Criticism. $17

HELEN BAROLINI. *Chiaroscuro: Essays of Identity*. Vol 11. Essays. $15

PICARAZZI & FEINSTEIN, Eds. *An African Harlequin in Milan*. Vol 10. Theater/Essays. $15

JOSEPH RICAPITO. *Florentine Streets & Other Poems*. Vol 9. Poetry. $9

FRED MISURELLA. *Short Time*. Vol 8. Novella. $7

NED CONDINI. *Quartettsatz*. Vol 7. Poetry. $7

ANTHONY JULIAN TAMBURRI, Ed. *Fuori: Essays by Italian/American Lesbiansand Gays*. Vol 6. Essays. $10

ANTONIO GRAMSCI. P. Verdicchio. Trans. & Intro. *The Southern Question*. Vol 5.Social Criticism. $5

DANIELA GIOSEFFI. *Word Wounds & Water Flowers*. Vol 4. Poetry. $8

WILEY FEINSTEIN. *Humility's Deceit: Calvino Reading Ariosto Reading Calvino*. Vol 3. Criticism. $10

PAOLO A. GIORDANO, Ed. *Joseph Tusiani: Poet. Translator. Humanist*. Vol 2. Criticism. $25

ROBERT VISCUSI. *Oration Upon the Most Recent Death of Christopher Columbus*. Vol 1. Poetry.

CPSIA information can be obtained
at www.ICGtesting.com
Printed in the USA
BVHW07s1410071018
529464BV00002B/39/P